ON THE HARDWOOD

BROOKLYN

ZACH WYNER

On the Hardwood: Brooklyn Nets

MVP Books
2255 Calle Clara
La Jolla, CA 92037

MVP Books is an imprint of Book Buddy Digital Media, Inc., 42982 Osgood Road, Fremont, CA 94539

MVP Books publications may be purchased for
educational, business, or sales promotional use.

Cover and layout design by Jana Ramsay
Copyedited by Susan Sylvia
Photos by Getty Images

ISBN: 978-1-61570-851-2 (Library Binding)
ISBN: 978-1-61570-835-2 (Soft Cover)

TABLE OF CONTENTS

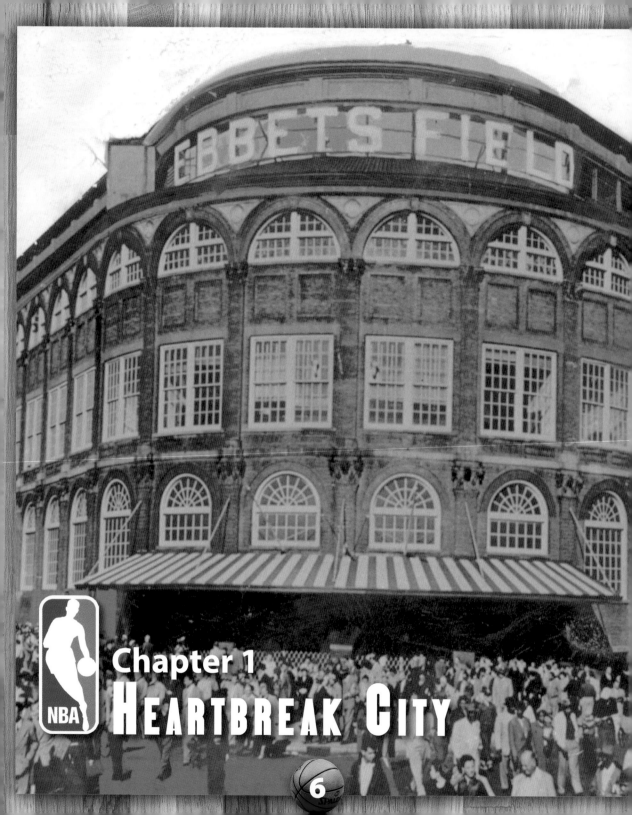

Chapter 1
HEARTBREAK CITY

Wait until next year. So goes the old saying. It's a hopeful saying, one you might hear spoken in barbershops, cafes, subway cars, and anywhere else that fans strike up a conversation about the local team that endured a painful losing season. It's only natural. Rather than focusing on their disappointment, fans comfort themselves with the promise of next year. Who knows what the future brings? Anything is possible... unless your team up and moves to California. In 1957, fans of the Brooklyn Dodgers experienced just that when their beloved baseball team relocated to Los Angeles. It would be over

50 years before those fans would get a chance to root for another professional sports team.

The relationship between a city and team may never have been

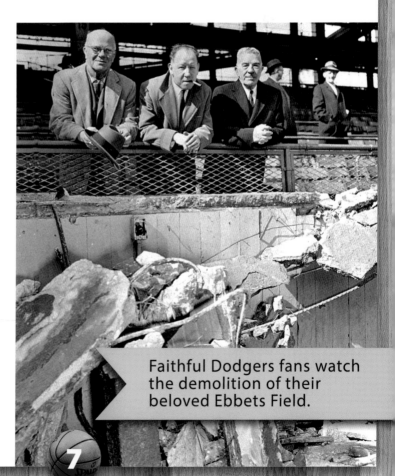

Faithful Dodgers fans watch the demolition of their beloved Ebbets Field.

Current Nets players pose with Dodger legends.

closer than the one between the Dodgers and Brooklyn. Existing in the shadow of Manhattan's towering skyscrapers, the city of Brooklyn was sometimes overlooked. To its residents, a diverse working-class community of immigrants from all over the world, the Dodgers were a unifying force. The players lived within blocks of the ballpark. During the offseason, they worked jobs in the neighborhood. Fans knew them by their first names. During the season, the people of Brooklyn gathered at Ebbets Field, located in the middle of the city, to cheer their hearts out. They cared about the Dodgers the way most people only care about family. When the Dodgers left, it tore a hole in the hearts of Brooklynites. Fifty-five years later, a professional basketball team called the Nets moved to Brooklyn to mend that hole.

Since the Nets were formed in 1967, they have called numerous locations in New York and New Jersey home. However, their most recent move to Brooklyn, a move that took nine years of planning, felt right. It felt inevitable. The story of the Nets is a story that resembles the city of Brooklyn itself. They've been put down, kicked around, and overshadowed by a world-famous neighbor. Just like Brooklyn, a world-famous neighbor has overshadowed the Nets. For decades, the New York Knicks and the Madison Square Garden outshined the Nets. For over a century, the bright lights of Manhattan outshined Brooklyn's rich diversity. But things change. And Brooklyn and the Nets are no longer content to live in the shadows.

Known earlier as the New Jersey Americans, the Nets were original members of the ABA (American Basketball Association). After one year in New Jersey, the team moved to Long Island, New York, and became the New York Nets. It was there that the team gained national recognition. But their sudden visibility had little to do with their new location. One man thrust the Nets into the spotlight—

the basketball genius known by the nickname "Dr. J." Remembered for his acrobatic, above-the-rim style of play, Julius "Dr. J" Erving helped the Nets become one of the most exciting basketball teams in any league. As a New York Net, he won the first ever slam-dunk contest, three straight MVP awards, and led the Nets to two ABA championships. In fact, he helped bring the ABA so much national attention that in 1976, the ABA and the NBA merged.

In 1976, four of the ABA's best teams (the Denver Nuggets, Indiana Pacers, San Antonio Spurs, and New York Nets) were allowed entry into the NBA. Before the start of their first NBA season, the Nets acquired Nate "Tiny" Archibald from the Kansas City Kings. With "Tiny" Archibald and Dr. J, many thought the Nets would not only compete in their new league, they would win championships. While this

Dr. J goes for the dunk against the Golden State Warriors.

development made Nets fans ec-static, it did not please the New York Knicks. The Knicks argued that the Nets were "invading" their base. Unfortunately for the Nets, the NBA agreed. The Nets were forced to pay a fine in order to stay in New York.

After paying the NBA's fine, the New York Nets could no longer af-ford their best player. Dr. J was traded to the Philadelphia 76ers, and a Nets team with so much promise, a team many thought capable of winning multiple championships, wound up in last place. That year would be their last year in New York. Due to poor attendance, the Nets were moved to New Jersey before the start of the 1977-78 season.

Over the next twenty years, the Nets and their fans saw glimmers

Dr. J shoots over Kurt Rambis and Kareem Abdul-Jabbar.

of hope. In 1984, they won their first NBA playoff series, eliminating the defending world champion Philadelphia 76ers in the first round. The victory was impressive. It came against their former star, Dr. J, and the reigning league MVP, Moses Malone. The Nets were led by Darryl "Chocolate Thunder" Dawkins, a

powerful 6'11", 250-pound power forward who many had been expecting great things from for years.

Called "the greatest high school player ever" by his varsity coach, Dawkins entered the NBA at the age of 18. In 1979, his legend grew when he shattered two backboards with a pair of devastating dunks during regular-season games. Gifted with a sense of humor nearly as entertaining as his slams, Dawkins named his backboard-breaking dunk, "The Chocolate-Thunder-Flying, Robinzine-Crying, Teeth-Shaking, Glass-Breaking, Rump-Roasting, Bun-Toasting, Wham-Bam, Glass-Breaker-I-Am-Jam." In fact, Dawkins came up with names for all of his dunks. Some of the more memorable names included "the Rim Wrecker," "the Go-Rilla," "the Look Out Below," "the In-Your-Face Disgrace," "the Cover Your Head," "the Yo-Mama," and "the Spine-Chiller Supreme."

But Chocolate Thunder and his high-flying, bun-toasting, glass-shattering jams were not enough to carry the Nets very far into the playoffs. After beating the 76ers in the first round, the Nets were defeated by the Milwaukee Bucks. In the years following their first playoff series victory, the Nets suffered a string of injuries that devastated a team and its once-hopeful fan base.

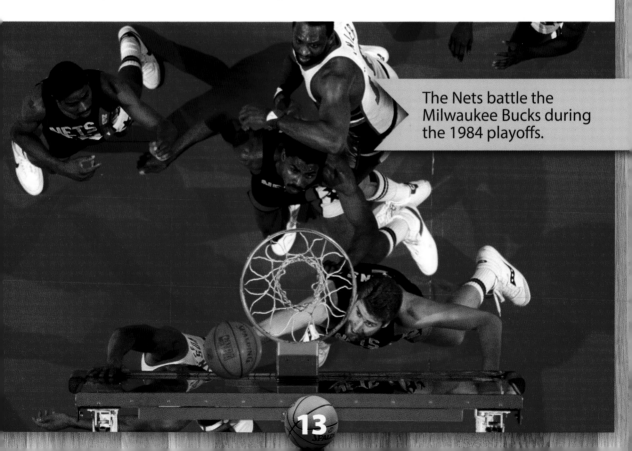

The Nets battle the Milwaukee Bucks during the 1984 playoffs.

Chapter 2

THAT KIDD CAN BALL

Darryl "Chocolate Thunder" Dawkins played two memorable seasons in New Jersey before a back injury robbed him of any chance at greatness. Never again would he be the rim-wrecking player he had been. Efforts were made to rebuild a team that had made the playoffs five straight seasons, but they didn't work. Eventually Chocolate Thunder was traded and the Nets suffered a long playoff drought.

In the early 1990s, the Nets climbed backed into contention around a trio of gifted players that included All-Stars Derrick Coleman and Kenny Anderson, and international superstar Drazen Petrovic.

Born in the former Yugoslavia (in what is now called Croatia),

Going Global

At the start of the 2012-13 season, a record-tying 84 international players from 37 different countries were on NBA team rosters.

Drazen Petrovic was a national hero before he ever set foot in the United States. A Croatian-born player who led Yugoslavia to gold medals at the European and World Championships, Petrovic (or "Petro" as he came to be known in New Jersey) possessed great energy, spirit, and one of the deadliest jump shots in the world. He joined the Portland Trail Blazers in 1989 at a time when it was still widely believed that European basketball players could not compete with NBA talent. For a season-and-a-half, Petro struggled to get consistent playing time, averaging between seven and 12 minutes per game. Then, during the 1990-91 season, he was traded to the Nets. At the time, few suspected that this under-the-radar trade would forever change the NBA.

The fiery Petrovic celebrates during Round 1 of the 1993 playoffs.

During his two full seasons with the Nets (1991-92 and 1992-93), Petro proved all his doubters wrong. He averaged over 20 points per game and led nearly all NBA guards by shooting over 50% from the field. Almost single-handedly, he began to change the way NBA management, players, and fans perceived international players. He became a fan favorite, and in 1993, he was named All-NBA Third Team and team MVP. Then tragedy struck. In the summer following the 1992-93 season, Petrovic traveled to Poland to play for the Croatian national team and was killed in an auto accident. He was only 28 years old. The Nets retired his number (3). Years later, in 2002, Petrovic was inducted into the Basketball Hall of Fame.

The tragic loss of a player, especially a team leader like Petrovic, is a very difficult thing for a team to overcome. The Nets persevered and made the playoffs in 1994, but in the years that followed, the team lost its way. Players like Derrick Coleman, Kenny Anderson, and Benoit Benjamin possessed great talent and athletic ability, but the team wasn't performing the way the experts thought it should. Players and fans were discouraged. Nets management had to make a decision; winning was no longer their biggest concern. The team's survival depended upon changing their image. Win or lose, they needed unselfish players who would compete together.

Changing the culture of a basketball team does not take place

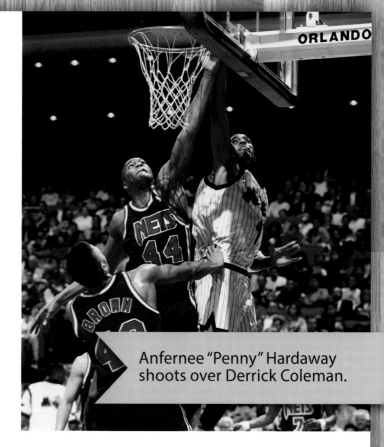

Anfernee "Penny" Hardaway shoots over Derrick Coleman.

Rebrand?
In 1994, in an attempt to alter the team's image, the Nets nearly changed their name to the New Jersey Swamp Dragons.

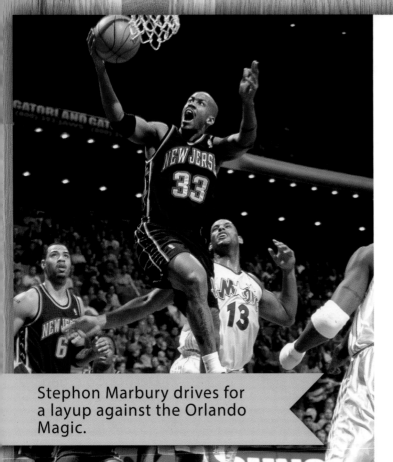

Stephon Marbury drives for a layup against the Orlando Magic.

A perfect example of a talented player who did not quite fit the team's new vision was Stephon Marbury. Marbury had been a high school legend in Coney Island, New York. When he was traded to the Nets from the Minnesota Timberwolves, both he and the fans were ecstatic. An explosive young scorer was coming home. From an individual standpoint, Marbury did not disappoint. During the 2000-01 season, he led the Nets with 24 points and 7.6 assists per game. But while Marbury was an incredible talent, he was not the leader that the Nets had been looking for. On the morning after the 2001 NBA Draft,

overnight. Transitions most often occur gradually. During the 1990s, the Nets dealt their former standouts piece by piece for draft picks and established talent.

From Brooklyn to Beijing

In 2012, Stephon Marbury led the Beijing Ducks to their first Chinese Basketball Association (CBA) title.

the Nets made the boldest move of a rebuilding process that had begun in 1996. They traded All-Star point guard and hometown hero Stephon Marbury to the Phoenix Suns for Jason Kidd.

By the time he arrived in New Jersey, there were very few comparisons in the history of the NBA to the 28-year-old Jason Kidd. A 6'4" floor general, he had very few holes in his game. He could score, rebound, defend, handle the ball, and he was already considered one of the game's all-time greatest passers. For six straight seasons he had averaged between nine and 11 assists per game. It was his ability to create good scoring opportunities for his teammates that the Nets desired most. With his trademark baseball pass, Kidd

Jason Kidd driving hard to the rim on a fast break.

Richard Jefferson shoots over a Celtic defender.

could ignite a fast break quicker than any other guard in the league. Combined with his ability to push the ball and finish at the rim, there was little other teams could do to slow down the suddenly turbocharged Nets.

In New Jersey, Kidd teamed up with a collection of strong, youthful players. Kenyon Martin, a fiery and explosive 6'9" power forward, dominated the boards and intimidated offenses with his length and shot-blocking ability. Keith Van Horn and Kerry Kittles could light things up from the outside, and the rookie, Richard Jefferson, was a scoring threat from anywhere on the floor. In Richard Jefferson, the Nets had a budding star who could shoot well from the outside as well as rain thunderous dunks down on the heads of helpless defenders. The addition of Jason Kidd to this lineup signaled hard times for the Nets' Eastern Conference foes. Hopeful fans did not have to wait long for the Kidd trade to pay off.

The Nets enjoyed the two best years in their history in 2002 and 2003. In the 2001-02 season, they won a franchise-record 52 games

and made the NBA Finals. In the finals, they were defeated by the powerful Los Angeles Lakers, but this disappointment only motivated them to try harder. The next year they came even closer to a championship. Again they finished the season as one of the top seeds

Kidd shoots over Derek Fisher in Game 1 of the 2002 NBA Finals.

It Takes Two to Tango

In 2002, Tim Duncan and Jason Kidd finished #1 and #2 in the voting for Most Valuable Player.

in the East and again they made it all the way to the NBA Finals. Waiting for them this time was Tim Duncan and the San Antonio Spurs.

Kenyon Martin and Manu Ginobili battle for the ball during the 2003 NBA Finals.

Trailing 2-1 in the series, the Nets won a gritty Game 4, 77-76. Jason Kidd had played stellar basketball throughout the playoffs, averaging 20 points, eight assists, and eight rebounds per game. In Game 4, the trio of Kidd, Martin, and Jefferson came through again, scoring 54 of the team's 77 points, while grabbing 31 rebounds and dishing out 13 assists. With one game left in New Jersey, it suddenly seemed possible that the Nets might upset the mighty Spurs. Unfortunately, Game 4 would be the last game the Nets would win that year. They lost the final two games of the series. They had come closer to an NBA title than any Nets team before them, but that knowledge did not prevent them from wondering what might have been.

After failing to make the NBA Finals in 2004, Nets management traded Kittles and Martin and brought Vince Carter to New Jersey. A new era was born, featuring a Kidd/Carter/Jefferson trio that many believed could put the Nets back in contention for a championship. Unfortunately for Nets fans, they were in for more disappointment. Kidd and Carter each made multiple All-Star teams, but the Kidd/Carter/Jefferson trio never went far into the playoffs.

By July of 2008, all the players that had led the 2003 Nets to

Kidd, Carter, and Jefferson pose for a team photo.

the NBA Finals were gone. Nets management was back to planning for the future, and Nets fans were asked to stay patient while the team went through another rebuilding process. Meanwhile, rumors that the team might be headed to a new home began to surface.

Chapter 3
BROOKLYN BROTHERHOOD

The history of sports in Brooklyn cannot be understood without grasping the city's relationship to the Dodgers. Brooklyn natives were like proud mothers and the Dodgers were their most adored child. The fact that this child didn't always win didn't matter. They loved it fiercely. Maybe even more so because it lost… a lot. Maybe that's what made it so sweet when it won. Maybe that's what made it so heartbreaking when it packed up and left home.

But baseball is not the only sport with deep roots in Brooklyn soil. The pounding of a basketball on asphalt has been—and still is—the heartbeat of this city. For decades, pick-up and high school basketball games have made

legends of local players.

The passing down of stories from one generation to the next is a tradition the world over. In Brooklyn, New York basketball fans have elevated this tradition to an art form. Local basketball stars, regardless of whether or not they make it all the way to the NBA, are

Deron Williams signs autographs for ecstatic fans.

25

not only followed, they're revered. Residents take pride in remembering players that the average NBA fan has never heard of; players whose playground or high school heroics became the stuff of legend. One such player, whose legend has refused to fade, is James "Fly" Williams.

Fly Williams had incredible hops. Despite his jumping ability, he never played in the NBA. But that fact doesn't stop many Brooklyn hoops fans from comparing him to Michael Jordan. Having first gained notoriety on Brooklyn's playgrounds and in its high school gymnasiums, Fly spent two memorable years at Austin Peay University in Tennessee.

As a freshman, he scored 30 points per game and led Austin Peay to the NCAA tournament. He followed that success up with one year in the ABA before his professional basketball career came to an abrupt end. Fly was a magnet for trouble. By the time he was in his early-twenties, he'd developed some bad habits and his priorities had changed. Sadly, Fly was unable to turn his life around in time for a shot at an NBA career. However, his story is one of redemption and hope. For the past twenty years, Fly has devoted his life to working with children at the Brownsville Recreation Center in Brooklyn, where his reputation as one of the city's greatest ballers is still intact.

The list of Brooklyn ballers who have made it to the NBA is longer,

Air Jordan's Brooklyn Roots

Michael Jordan was born in Brooklyn but moved to Wilmington, North Carolina, when he was a toddler.

and arguably more impressive, than any other city in the United States. Players such as Lenny Wilkins, Albert King, Doug Moe, Connie Hawkins, Billy Cunningham, World B. Free, Chris Mullin, Mark Jackson, Bernard King, Stephon Marbury, and the player that might one day stand above them all, Carmelo Anthony, all grew up playing on the public courts or in the high schools of Brooklyn. These players not only carry the city of Brooklyn in their hearts, they also played (and continue to play) with a style rooted in their hometown.

In the 2012 Olympics, Carmelo Anthony averaged 16.3 points per game, helping the U.S.A. bring home the gold medal.

Before the Internet and national TV broadcasts, the game of basketball looked different in different cities. Players were influenced by what they saw at local parks, not by what was on SportsCenter or YouTube. The games played at Kelly Miller Park in Washington, D.C., or at Mosswood Park in Oakland, California, looked different from the games played in Brooklyn. In fact, Brooklyn ballers will tell you that

McCarran Park, Brooklyn

their game was different even from the style of game being played just across the East River at legendary Rucker Park in Harlem, New York.

The Brooklyn game started early in the morning and continued throughout the day. At most parks they played four-on-four as opposed to five-on-five. This created a wide-open court with more room to move, run, and improvise. But don't think that this meant the game was softer. You called your own fouls, but fouls were rarely if ever called. Pushing and shoving were allowed. And if you lost, you sat on the sidelines and waited (sometimes for hours) for your turn to get back on the court. As you watched and waited, you silently passed your ball between your legs or fiddled with the change you kept hidden in your sock. It was this world that birthed legend upon legend, and eventually changed the way basketball was played everywhere.

Hoops Heaven

Foster Park and street ball legend "Fly" Williams were the focus of Rick Telander's classic book, *Heaven Is a Playground*.

Two of the most notable players birthed by the courts of Brooklyn were Bernard and Albert King. While they were in high school, it was believed that Albert might be the best player to ever come out of Brooklyn. However, an inch taller and 15 pounds heavier than Albert, it was older brother Bernard that had the size to dominate in the NBA. The first team he played for was none other than the New Jersey Nets. In his rookie season, Bernard averaged 24 points and 10 rebounds. After a second season that saw his numbers dip slightly, the Nets decided to trade him. It was a move they would come to regret. Bernard King went on to make three All-Star teams and win a scoring title in 1985. Most experts agree that, if not for a devastating knee injury, Bernard King would be remembered as one of the greatest offensive players in league history.

After leaving the Knicks, Bernard spent time with the Warriors and the Jazz before returning to the East Coast. It was as a member of the New York Knicks that he would become a Hall-of-Fame caliber player. It was also as a member of the Knicks that he would play in some memorable

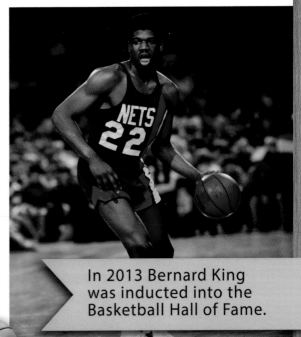

In 2013 Bernard King was inducted into the Basketball Hall of Fame.

battles against his former team, a team that included a very familiar face.

The 1982-83 New Jersey Nets were not to be taken lightly. With Daryl Dawkins, Otis Birdsong, Buck Williams, and Michael Ray Richardson, the Nets had their best team since joining the NBA. In addition to these standouts, starting at small forward (and enjoying the best season of his career) was Bernard's younger brother, Albert King. Playing in the Atlantic Division, home to Bernard King's Knicks, Dr. J's Philadelphia 76ers, and Larry Bird's Boston Celtics, the Nets faced a steady stream of fierce competition. And yet, under coach Larry Brown, they won 49 regular-season games and earned the fourth seed in the Eastern Conference playoffs. There was reason for hope in New Jersey.

That hope was dashed the day Larry Brown accepted the head coaching position at the University of Kansas. Two weeks before the playoffs were set to begin, Brown quit his job and the Nets were forced to start over with a new leader. The two-game

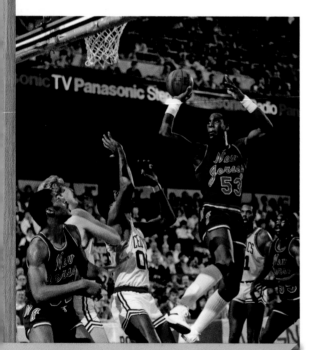

Darryl Dawkins attempts an acrobatic shot over Robert Parish of the Boston Celtics.

playoff series that pitted brother against brother was not without its drama. But the Nets were unable to play with the cohesion and focus that had earned them home-court advantage against their crosstown rivals.

Albert King uses his impressive wingspan to prevent the inbounds pass.

In Game 1 of the 1983 playoffs, Bernard and Albert King squared off against one another in one of the biggest basketball games since the Nets had moved to New Jersey. Each led their team in scoring. Unfortunately for the Nets, Albert's 17 points did not come close to matching Bernard's 40.

Game 2, played in New York, was much closer. This time Albert led both teams with 25 points while Darryl Dawkins and Buck Williams each poured in 22 of their own. But five New York players scored in double figures and the Knicks eked out a narrow six-point victory. Bernard's Knicks had earned themselves temporary bragging rights. However, it was the city of Brooklyn, watching two native sons compete on the basketball's biggest stage that had truly won the day.

Chapter 4
A Dynamic Duo

Brooklyn street and high school basketball turned teenagers into local heroes. Local heroes like Bernard King blossomed into national legends. But cities that produce great talent are not guaranteed a professional basketball team. Precious few cities in the country are lucky enough to host an NBA team. Although Brooklyn once proved itself to be a city of passionate and dedicated fans, more than 50 years had gone by since the Dodgers left for Los Angeles. And those 50 years had not always been kind to Brooklyn. The city had (and still has) its share of poverty. Unfortunately, professional sports teams require more than a dedicated and passionate fan base. They require a fan base that can afford to buy lots of tickets. If a city cannot financially support a professional sports team, no team is going to come. None of this stopped Nets ownership from believing a move to Brooklyn was possible.

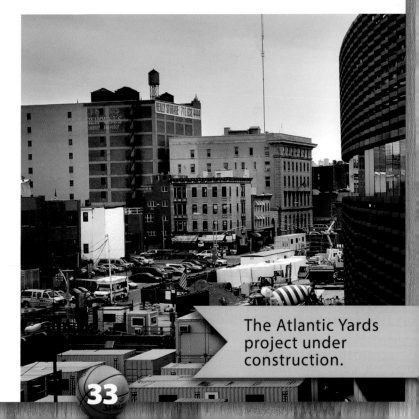

The Atlantic Yards project under construction.

Mikhail Prokhorov and Jay-Z discuss their business venture.

In order to make the dream of moving to Brooklyn a reality, the Nets would need to attract an ambitious owner. This meant finding someone who had already been successful in the business world but was still hungry for a challenge. It meant finding someone with lots of money, but it also meant finding someone who was competitive and willing to take a risk. In Mikhail Prokhorov and Jay-Z, the Nets found the people they needed: a dynamic duo (one from the other side of the globe and one from Brooklyn's own Bedford-Stuyvesant district) that would bring attention, money, and a story as irresistible as the city itself.

Even the greatest players on earth need to be surrounded by

an outstanding supporting cast if they hope to win a championship. Without Dwyane Wade, LeBron James never won a title; without Ray Allen and Paul Pierce, Kevin Garnett only made it as far as the Western Conference Finals. Knowing this to be true, basketball stars want to play for owners who hate to lose as much as they do, owners who are willing to invest money to surround their stars with talent. In Mikhail Prokhorov, the Nets had not merely found a businessman who was willing to spend, they found a competitor with an intense desire to win.

Mikhail Prokhorov is one of the richest and most talked-about owners in the NBA. Standing 6'8" tall, he is as tall or taller than many of the Nets players. And he is every

Prokhorov attends a basketball training session at a secondary school in Moscow.

bit as devoted an athlete. Prokhorov is an avid jet-skier who performs back flips on his stand-up jet ski, and he is president of the Russian

Money Talks

With a net worth of over $13 billion, Prokhorov was listed by Forbes magazine as the 58th richest man in the world in 2012.

Aiming High

Prokhorov hopes to bring Brooklyn its first professional sports title since the Dodgers won the Word Series in 1955.

Biathlon Union (a biathlon is a sport that combines cross-country skiing and target shooting). In addition to his sporting and business activities, Prokhorov is a politician and head of the Civic Platform Party (a small new political party that wants to help develop business in Russia). Clearly he is a busy man with a lot on his plate! But his frantic schedule has not stopped him from putting a great deal of time and energy into his American basketball team.

When Mikhail Prokhorov bought the Nets, he became the first Russian-born owner in the history of the NBA. But that wasn't the only history Prokhorov was interested in making. Brimming with confidence, he guaranteed Brooklyn a championship within five years. In addition

Prokhorov takes in Nets training camp with coaches and players.

Shovels are lined up for the Atlantic Yards ceremonial groundbreaking.

BARCLAYS CENTER
ATLANTIC YARDS

BARCLAYS CENTER
ATLANTIC YARDS

Ceremonial
Groundbreaking

March 11, 2010

to that promise, he and a New York developer made another promise to residents of the city: let us build Barclay's Center (the arena where the Nets play their home games) and we will also develop the community around it. The building project was called Atlantic Yards.

Nets ownership proposed building the Barclay's Center in a neighborhood called Prospect Heights. As excited as most Brooklyn residents were for the Nets' arrival, people did not want to see the residents of Prospect Heights swept aside to make room for a basketball team. Prokhorov promised Brooklyn that if permitted to build a sports arena in Prospect Heights, he would also build affordable housing, retail, and office complexes.

While these promises all sounded good, the people of Brooklyn had reason to be skeptical that the

Nets would be good for their town. Historically speaking, the team was a losing franchise. They might have a new owner with deep pockets, but wealth alone does not make a winner. What if the team stunk? What if tickets didn't sell? How many new jobs would there be in Atlantic Yards if no one showed up to watch the games? What the Nets needed was someone whose mere presence could transform their image. They needed someone who could make them cool and glamorous, someone that basketball players and New Yorkers both respected and admired. Enter Jay-Z.

Born Shawn Carter in 1969 in Brooklyn, Jay-Z rose from the public housing projects of Bedford-Stuyvesant to become one of the most successful self-made businessmen in the country. His success was a testament to his strength and determination, qualities that he credits to his hometown. But these qualities alone did not take Jay-Z to the top of the rap game. The Brooklyn native also happens to be hugely talented. His albums *Reasonable Doubt* and *The Blueprint* are on *Rolling Stone Magazine's* list of 500 Greatest Albums of All Time. In addition to this, Jay-Z is the former CEO of Def Jam recordings, has received 14 Grammy awards, and in 2006, he was ranked #1 by MTV in their list of The Greatest MCs of All-Time.

Two Stars for the Price of One

By bringing Jay-Z into the family, the Nets also brought his wife, Beyonce Knowles, with him.

In Jay-Z, Prokhorov found a partner who could generate the excitement needed to get the media buzzing. With the media now paying extra attention to the Nets, the players did too. Suddenly the NBA's best free agents (a player whose contract with their current team is about to end) were including the Nets on short lists of teams they'd like to play for. The first step in the transformation of the Nets had begun. They were on their way to becoming a team that competed for championships, a team that kids, streetballers, and high school players would dream of playing for.

Jay-Z and wife Beyonce Knowles take in the action from their courtside seats.

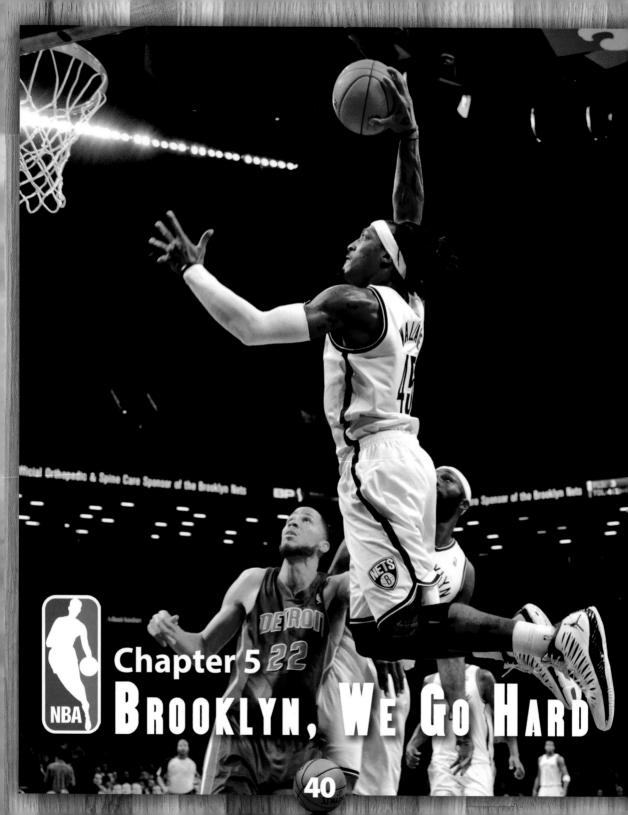

Chapter 5
BROOKLYN, WE GO HARD

The New Jersey Nets finished the 2010-11 season near the bottom of the Eastern Conference. Their record was 24-58. It was the end of a painful year during which the team lost 18 straight games and failed to attract any of the 2003 NBA Draft class from signing with them. Despite Prokhorov's and Jay-Z's best efforts, LeBron James, Chris Bosh, and Dwyane Wade all signed with the Miami Heat. Also, after pushing hard to bring local-hero-turned-national-superstar Carmelo Anthony to their squad, Carmelo was traded to the New York Knicks. But the Nets didn't give up. The week after the Carmelo trade

A happy Deron Williams poses with his new uniform.

fell through, they acquired All-Star point guard Deron Williams from the Utah Jazz. Bothered by a wrist injury, Williams was forced to sit out many of the team's remaining games, but the Nets stayed hopeful. They believed that Williams and their

A healthy Brook Lopez, shooting over LeBron James in the post.

young, offensively-gifted center, Brook Lopez, could make a powerful duo. They hoped that the team's last year in New Jersey would be one to build on.

Unfortunately for the Nets, the 2011-12 lockout-shortened season began with more bad luck. Brook Lopez suffered a stress fracture in his foot that kept him out most of the season. Deron Williams performed well, averaging 21 points per game, but his assists dropped to just over eight per game (one fewer than his career average). Deron needed help. In February of 2012, help began to arrive in the form of Gerald Wallace. An 11-year veteran of the league, the 6'7" Wallace had made the All-Star team for the first time in 2010 as a member of the Charlotte

Bobcats. Known early in his career for his explosive dunks, Wallace had developed into a consistent scorer, rebounder, and an outstanding defender.

Gerald Wallace brought added skill and experience to the Nets, but the 2011-12 season could not be rescued. Demoralized by injuries, the team struggled through the final games of a disappointing season. On April 23rd, 2012, the Nets played their last game in New Jersey before a sell-out crowd. They lost to the Philadelphia 76ers by 18 points. For the fans, it was a tough way to end an era that had been filled with letdowns. The New Jersey Nets had enjoyed some terrific seasons, but the majority of

Gerald Wallace protects the rim against All-Star point guard, Kyrie Irving.

their time in the Garden State had been painful. Tragedy, injuries and suspensions each played a part in preventing the New Jersey Nets from

The Second Season
While playing in New Jersey, the Nets made the playoffs 16 times and twice made it all the way to the NBA Finals.

Fans browse in the team shop at the Barclays Center before a home game.

officially became the Brooklyn Nets and their new Jay-Z designed logo was unveiled. Fans flocked to stores to buy new jackets, jerseys, and caps. In fact, Brooklyn Nets gear outsold every other NBA team in the opening months of the 2012-13 season. But uniform sales were not the kind of triumph that Nets ownership had had in mind when they relocated.

While the Nets players were eager to start over in Brooklyn, Brooklyn fans wondered what kind of a team was coming to their city. Sportswriters doubted whether the change of location and uniforms would make any difference in the Nets' fortunes. But Nets ownership, coaches, and players were confident

being consistently competitive. The time had come for a change.

On April 30th, 2012, the Nets

Fashion Statement

The Nets new logo was designed to remind fans of NYC subway signs from the 1950s when Brooklyn last had a professional team.

that things were going to get better. The spring and summer of 2012 showed the basketball world just how serious the Nets were about getting better fast.

November 3rd, 2012, will be remembered as the day that the Brooklyn Nets won their first game, a home opener against the Toronto Raptors, 107-100. However, it was on a balmy summer day four months earlier that the Nets enjoyed their biggest victory since Jason Kidd led them to the NBA Finals. It didn't matter that on that day no basketball was played.

On July 11th, 2012, with two moves, the Brooklyn Nets signaled the arrival of a new day for the franchise. The first move was a trade for six-time All-Star Joe Johnson from the Atlanta Hawks. The second was the signing of Deron Williams to a five-year deal worth nearly $100 million. Johnson and Williams became the two premiere pieces of what Nets management called their

Joe Johnson and Deron Williams make one of the most explosive duos in the NBA.

"Core Four" – Deron Williams, Joe Johnson, Gerald Wallace, and Brook Lopez. With this core, the Nets had assembled a group of players that could immediately compete for a division title.

For a number of years the New Jersey Nets were a team on life support. Like a patient with a weak heart, they struggled to survive long, injury-riddled seasons. Time and again, they staggered into the playoffs or missed them altogether. Time and again, fans were left hoping for a better season next year. In November of 2012, that better year arrived. The patient got a transplant. Brooklyn's heartbeat—a basketball bouncing on the city's sidewalks, echoing in its high school gymnasiums, pounding the asphalt courts of its public parks— infused the Nets players with re- newed energy and spirit. The team responded, giving their new fans something to cheer for.

The 2012 Brooklyn Nets' starting five.

In the Nets' first month in Brooklyn, the team went 11-4. Brook Lopez returned from his foot injury to lead the team with 19 points and 2.5 blocks per game. Deron Williams and Joe Johnson each scored a shade under 16 points per game, and Williams led the team in assists per game with nine. Gerald Wallace played his typical great defense and led the team in steals. But the real surprise was the Nets bench. Reggie Evans, a physical power forward, led them with nine rebounds per game in only 20 minutes of playing time. In addition, newly acquired power forward Andray Blatche and veteran swingman Jerry Stackhouse provided a serious offensive boost.

In 2012, the Brooklyn Nets were welcomed to their new home and they came out firing. But perhaps the most impressive part of their hot start was that a team with so many new players could play together so well, so soon. Ordinarily it takes time for a team to gel. Players

Reggie Evans throws down a dunk against the Washington Wizards.

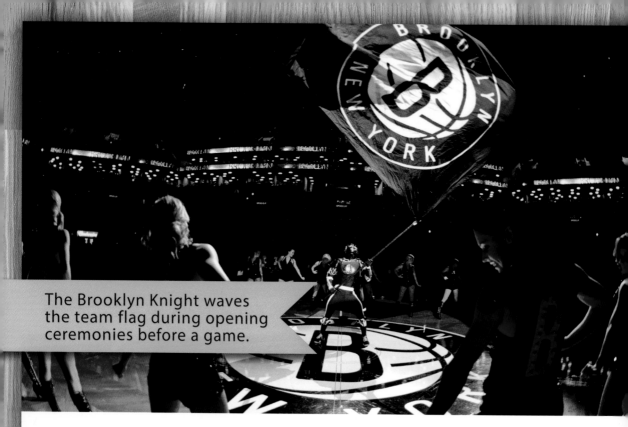

The Brooklyn Knight waves the team flag during opening ceremonies before a game.

must be patient, unselfish and learn each other's strengths and weaknesses. They must be willing to sacrifice. Sometimes that means playing fewer minutes or focusing on defense. Sometimes it means settling for fewer jump shots and driving the ball to the rim. If the first month of the 2012-13 season was any indication of how well the Nets will adjust to their new roles and new city, Brooklyn has good reason to be excited. And excited is something they deserve to be. After all, they only waited 55 years for this moment. In the words of Jay-Z, "Let it ring out, it's a warning, BROOKLYN! Let it be sworn in." NBA teams beware; the Nets and the city of Brooklyn go hard.